D0759191

If you were a

Comma

by Molly Blaisdell   illustrated by Sara Gray

WITHDRAWN

PICTURE WINDOW BOOKS
Minneapolis, Minnesota

comma (,) a punctuation mark used to separate words, groups of words, or numbers

Editors: Christianne Jones and Jill Kalz
Designer: Tracy Davies
Page Production: Melissa Kes
Art Director: Nathan Gassman
Editorial Director: Nick Healy
The illustrations in this book were created with acrylics.

Picture Window Books
151 Good Counsel Drive
P.O. Box 669
Mankato, MN 56002-0669
877-845-8392
www.picturewindowbooks.com

Copyright © 2009 by Picture Window Books
All rights reserved. No part of this book may be reproduced
without written permission from the publisher. The publisher
takes no responsibility for the use of any of the materials or
methods described in this book, nor for the products thereof.

Printed in the United States of America.

All books published by Picture Window Books
are manufactured with paper containing at least
10 percent post-consumer waste.

Library of Congress Cataloging-in-Publication Data
Blaisdell, Molly, 1964–
If you were a comma / by Molly Blaisdell ; illustrated by
Sara Gray.
p. cm. — (Word Fun)
Includes index.
ISBN 978-1-4048-5320-1 (library binding)
ISBN 978-1-4048-5321-8 (paperback)
1. English language—Punctuation—Juvenile literature.
2. Comma—Juvenile literature. 3. North Pole—Juvenile
literature. 4. Language arts (Primary) I. Gray, Sara, ill.
II. Title.
PE1450.B63 2009
428.2—dc22   2008039312

Looking for commas?

Watch for the BIG marks throughout the book.

Special thanks to our advisers for their expertise:
Rosemary G. Palmer, Ph.D., Department of Literacy
College of Education, Boise State University

Terry Flaherty, Ph.D., Professor of English
Minnesota State University, Mankato

If you were a comma ...

3

... you could take a trip to the North Pole.

You could pack
your bags,

jump on an airplane,

and fly off on an adventure!

If you were a comma, you could separate a series of single words.

The northern lights are colorful, bright, flickering, and wavy.

The crowd gasps, cheers, and claps at the beautiful display.

If you were a comma, you could separate a series of word groups.

Miki Musk Ox glided across a glacier,

sailed around an iceberg,

and hiked over the frozen ground.

Miki built an igloo,

skated on an ice floe,

and sledded down a hill.

If you were a comma, you could separate a series of actions.

Patsy Polar Bear loves snowshoeing, skiing, and dogsledding.

She does not like
cooking, cleaning,
and washing laundry.

If you were a comma, you could separate a series of names.

Miguel chooses Walter, Roxie, and Harry for his team. Patsy, Cleo, and Flip will play for the other team.

If you were a comma, you could connect two sentences that go together. You would need help from a coordinating conjunction, such as *and*, *but*, or *so*.

The North Pole has 24 hours of daylight in summer,

and it has 24 hours of nighttime in winter.

15

If you were a comma, you could be
a part of a large number.

The Reindeer family loves to count stars.

Russ Reindeer
counts
1,870 stars.

Roxie Reindeer counts 11,545 stars.

Randy Reindeer counts 100,000 stars.

If you were a comma, you would be an important part of every letter. You would separate the day from the year. You would follow the greeting and the closing.

January 11, 2010

Dear Mom,
It's dark and cold here.

Love,
Miguel

If you were a comma, you would help a letter get to its location. You would separate the city from the state.

Miguel Gator
10 Chilly Lane
North Pole

Mrs. Allie Gator
411 Citrus Street
Sunville, FL 77777

You could put together photos of ice, lights, and nice new friends ...

... if you were a comma.

Quick Review

Commas are used to separate a series of single words.

Miguel takes pictures of bears, puffins, and moose.

Commas are also used to separate a series of word groups.

Patsy played hockey, skiied down a hill, and started a snowball fight.

A comma works with a coordinating conjunction to join sentences that go together.

Walter played goalie, and Roxie played center.

Commas are used in large numbers.

Cleo's grandma lives 1,000 miles away.

A comma follows the greeting and closing in a letter.

Dear Harry,   Your friend,

Commas separate days from years and cities from states.

May 15, 2011   Fairbanks, Alaska

Fun with Commas

Gather a group of friends. Give each person a pen and a page from an old magazine.

Now take 30 seconds to circle as many commas as you can. Ask an adult to time you. The person with the most commas at the end of the 30 seconds wins!

Glossary

comma—a punctuation mark used to separate
   words, groups of words, or numbers
coordinating conjunction—a two- or three-letter
   word that joins sentences or parts of sentences
punctuation—marks used to make written
   language clear
separate—to set apart
series—a number of things coming one
   after another

To Learn More

More Books to Read

Pulver, Robin. *Punctuation Takes a Vacation.* New York:
   Holiday House, 2003.
Salzmann, Mary Elizabeth. *Comma.* Edina, Minn.: ABDO
   Pub., 2001.
Truss, Lynne. *Eats, Shoots & Leaves: Why, Commas Really
   Do Make a Difference!* New York: G.P. Putnam's Sons, 2006.

On the Web

FactHound offers a safe, fun way to find educator-approved
Internet sites related to this book.

Here's what you do:
   1. Visit *www.facthound.com*
   2. Choose your grade level.
   3. Begin your search.

This book's ID number is 9781404853201

Index

Look for all of the books in the Word Fun: Punctuation series:

If You Were a Comma
If You Were a Period
If You Were a Question Mark
If You Were an Apostrophe
If You Were an Exclamation Point
If You Were Quotation Marks